SEARCHING FOR SOLACE

Dealing With My Father's Sucide

Ilana Greenstein

cover design – David Cowan
cover photo – Rebecca Jereza

The **Ilana Typeface** was developed by Tobin Strong of
www.fontgrill.com based on Ilana's handwriting. She wrote out
the letters of the alphabet and several sentences to show what her
handwriting looks like on paper, and Tobin created it into a font.
This way, her book can look as much like her actual journal as
possible.

ISBN – 10: 1-56499-082-6

ISBN – 13: 978-1-56499-082-2

INNERCHOICE Publishing
15079 Oak Chase Court
Wellington, FL 33414

www.InnerchoicePublishing.com

DEDICATION

To Michele Kennedy, for always being there when I needed her and never giving up on me.

To Mary Palisoul, for her kindness and compassion, and the way she drove me to love writing more than I ever had before.

To the Ellisons, for welcoming me with open arms and making me feel completely at home.

And to Kayla Shore, for being the best friend I could ever ask for.

ACKNOWLEDGMENTS

I would like to thank my mom for providing constant support, encouragement, and love; my sister for always putting a smile on my face; Susanna for being the most delightful, kind, and talented publisher I could ever dream of working with; Julie for taking the time to edit my book; all my friends and teachers for understanding and caring about me; and lastly, the Shores for being my second family and loving me through everything. All of you mean so much to me and I can't begin to tell you how much you've helped me throughout this whole process, but I can say that I love you all enormously.

The Beginning

Have you ever heard the saying, "Every obstacle presents an opportunity to improve one's condition"? Although it may be extremely hard to believe this statement at times, it's always true in the long run. Almost two years ago, my dad committed suicide and I felt like my life was crashing down before me. I was 15 years old, a sophomore in high school, and things like that don't just happen. But it did. Even though everything seemed to fall apart, I was able to piece my life back together and heal with the help of my friends, family, and writing. Writing is my escape- it's the way I deal with all the pressures around me. In this book, I've shared my journal that I kept in the year following my dad's death in hopes that you will be able to use it as a starting point for your own healing process. I've included prompts throughout the book relating to issues I had to face so that you can give your own input and apply the situations to your life.

You may find that writing isn't the most effective way for you to deal with whatever loss you're facing, and that's okay. Maybe painting is your escape, or singing, or running, or anything else that allows you to feel completely safe and free. The healing process is not a smooth progression; there will always be ups and downs, and that's perfectly normal. But there will also always be something that can help you pull through. Every person has his or her own escape, and through reading my journal and working through the prompts, I hope you can begin to find yours.

This is the eulogy I read at my dad's funeral:

On Monday at 3:00, my friend Caroline and I walked to my house. I had forgotten my key, so I rang the doorbell and called the house phone. I saw that my dad's car was there, but he wasn't picking up the phone, so I went to Caroline's house with her. From Caroline's house I went to baby-sit, and was a little worried about my dad so I left my mom a message. When I got home from baby-sitting, my mom got home at the same time and she let us in. When we came up the stairs, I saw a sticky note on Dad's computer. It had tons of words on it, but the only ones I saw were "suicide note". I screamed and my mom looked at the note and went upstairs. She came down seconds later and said, "I need to call 9-1-1!"

The next few hours are a blur to me. I screamed, cried, and was brought to my friend's house so I didn't have to see the body being taken downstairs. I was angry, sad, distressed, shocked, and full of disbelief. The next day was even worse.

I tried to keep everything inside but I had so many thoughts whirling through my head.

I am so mad at my dad. If I had had my key, I would have been the one to find the body, and my mom wouldn't have been able to come home for an hour. How could he kill himself? How could he be so selfish? My sister was about to take her exams, and now she had to come right home and take them later. His father and stepmother had just flown out to California, and now they had to come back here. He put my mother, my sister, me, and all of our friends and family through so much pain.

But he was in pain. His whole life, he was suffering and hurting. By killing himself he finally ended his suffering. I pity my dad for not being able to ever find the joy in life, not ever being fully satisfied, not ever burden free.

Although I have never believed in this before, I find myself picturing my dad up in heaven. He can't see the world, can't see pain, suffering, grief--he is in his own, pain-free world, finally content and happy. The way he left this world was horrible and terrifying, but I am glad he is, at last, set free.

Wednesday, December 16

My dad killed himself exactly one month ago.

My dad died a month ago.

My dad passed away 30 days ago.

No matter how I say it, it still somehow doesn't seem real. I know it happened, but I can't grasp it. I still think, 'What time is Dad picking me up today?', 'I wonder how Dad will be today', 'Dad would really like...'

Some days I feel totally normal. I'm happy, distracted, and content. I think about him frequently, but there isn't a dark shadow that seems to encompass me when I do so.

Other days, the shadow lurks within me all day long. Everything everybody says reminds me of him. When I go into a dark, empty room, he is there, giving me a solemn, cold stare. It makes me shiver.

When I'm alone, I remember the day he died. I try to imagine what could have been running through his mind, something so unbelievably powerful as to make him give up his wife, children, parents, and whole family instantly. Something so unfathomable and wretched that he didn't even think about the effect on my sister, my mother, me, and everyone who loved and cared about him. I was supposed to come home first, I was supposed to find him ...

There are no "supposed tos", my mom says. So maybe I wasn't "supposed to" find him.

He wasn't "supposed to" kill himself, either.

Saturday, December 19

When I think about my dad I instantly think about the last few months: the yelling, the crying, the fighting. I have to put in extra effort to remember the good things.

When I was young, sliding around an icy, empty parking lot in his car.

Tickle fights with him, my sister, and me.

Playing cards on his bed for hours.

Going to the arcade on a Saturday afternoon.

Pretending to be at a restaurant and serving him gourmet meals consisting of whatever was in the refrigerator, and charging him $0.02 for it.

I just had a flashback to last Monday in school. It was the end of History, and we were about to wrap up. We were talking about government and its role in people's affairs, and before I knew it, someone brought up suicide.

"Should the government interfere if someone's going to kill himself?"

"You can't really stop someone from killing himself."

"If they're gonna do it, they're gonna do it."

"If someone is that messed up the government can't do anything about it ..."

I froze. My face and body felt really hot and I felt like I was stuck. Everyone starting packing up, putting their things away and their backpacks on, and all I could do was sit and stare straight ahead of me. My friend Kayla asked if I was all right, and I slowly shook my head. She helped me up, and we went to my counselor's office. On the door was a note that said she would be gone all day. Kayla and I went to the bathroom, locked the door to the handicap stall, and hugged while I cried into her shoulder. I had English next, so Kayla took me to my English teacher's office. She came in, saw me crying, and gave me a big hug. I managed to tell her what happened.

"Is that the way your father died?" she asked slowly.

I nodded, and she hugged me again. She took me to the guidance director, whom I had never met before. I sat with her and told her everything. She was really nice and understanding, and by the end of the period I felt better.

What do you think?

Even after a difficult experience, like having people talk about suicide right in front of me, talking to someone about the situation made me feel a lot better. Sometimes it's hard to open up to people, but talking out your problem can really help you to understand exactly what you're feeling and why.

Who can *you* talk to? What would *you* say?

Sunday, December 27

On Friday night, I had the worst dream of my life. I was sitting across from Dad at the dining room table, and he was yelling horrible things at me. Then he started throwing things at me, like food and dishes from the table. He threw a plate at me and it shattered on my feet. I was yelling to my mom but she was on the phone and wasn't paying attention to me. He kept throwing things at me. I went and hid in the pantry, and he yelled at me through the door. I kept yelling "Mom! Mom!" but she was busy on the phone. I escaped from the pantry and ran to my mom. Dad was about to leave, and he said to me, "Next time, I'm going to kill you."

Mom took me to my therapist yesterday. My therapist doesn't work on Saturdays, but wanted to meet with me because this was an emergency. She said the dreams reflected feelings I had about my dad, the fear and horror. She prescribed me a sleep medicine, and also Mom and I started a bedtime ritual. My mom sits on the end of my bed and reads me poems so that I can get good thoughts into my head before I go to sleep. I didn't have any bad dreams last night, so I guess it's working so far.

What do you think?

Consciously thinking good thoughts can help relieve stress and tension. What are some good thoughts you've had?

Wednesday, December 30

I think often of the intervention. When I was in eighth grade, my dad was very addicted to poker. He started playing at higher and higher stakes, and he lost hundreds of thousands of dollars. My mom decided that she had to do something, so she met with a counselor to help plan an intervention.

The night of the play that I had helped to stage manage, my mom told my sister and me about her plans. I started crying hysterically. Dad was either going to have to go to an addiction treatment home, or my mom would kick him out. My friend Kayla went to the play with me and supported me through it.

About a week later, my mom took my sister and me to the counselor, and together we called my grandparents to tell them about the intervention. I couldn't stop crying. My mom had tried to shield me as much as she could from how awful things were, but now the worst of it was coming out. My dad was addicted to other things too, besides the poker, but I didn't know they were related. The addiction, according to my dad, was caused by a certain drug he was taking. Many people who took the drug had similar episodes and also gambled uncontrollably. My mom doesn't think the drug caused his behaviors, though.

At the intervention, we sat around in the living room. We were all supposed to prepare something to say, even my grandparents. Everyone spoke before me and told my dad how his addiction had negatively affected him or her. I was last, and I quietly said how when I brought friends home and he was in a bad mood, it wasn't fun. Then my dad spoke for nearly an hour about how it was the drug's fault, not his, and how no one understood him. My mom told him his two options, but he convinced her to let him stay and not go to an addiction treatment center. He stayed, and kept playing poker. And kept losing money.

My parents drew up a contract that said my dad had to be a nicer person and put $6,000 in my parents' bank account every month. He kept up with it for a while (the money part, not the nicer person part), but in the last few months he wasn't putting anything in the bank.

After the intervention, my dad gave me a hug, but I didn't feel any emotional connection to him. I felt completely detached in a way I had never felt before. I did not love him anymore. I had to get out of the house, but I didn't have anywhere to go. I ended up sitting on our swing set for almost two hours until Kayla came home and I could go to her house. I slept at her house that night.

My mom often tells me how clearly she remembers what I said to her after the intervention, something I don't remember. I said to her, "Mom, it's not the poker, it's him." She says that she couldn't see it then, but I was completely right, and my words made a big difference in the way she thought about our family thereafter.

What do you think?

The intervention changed my feelings about my dad in a huge way; I saw a totally different side of him that I hadn't come in contact with before. Have you ever had an experience that made you greatly change your opinion of someone? Write about the situation, and how your relationship with that person changed because of it.

Sunday, January 10

How many people know? Do they all know, and they just don't want to talk about it? I want to talk about it, want to scream about it. Everyone walks on eggshells around me. They don't know how I'm going to feel in a given day, hour, minute. It changes so quickly. I can't keep up with my own head.

The spring and summer before Dad killed himself, he was in the worst pain of his life. He was bed-ridden, solemn, and miserable. Seeing him made me solemn too, for he was like a darkness that engulfed everyone and everything around him. In the summer, when I was home for most of the day, I was his slave, fetching him things constantly. He was a deep pit of neediness, never filled to contentment. There was always something he needed, wanted, but couldn't have.

He said to me one day, "Ilana, I wish you were more caring." I responded, "Dad, I've been so caring to you." He replied, "Sometimes you are. But sometimes I feel like you don't understand me or care for me."

I got so mad at him. No matter what I, my mom, or anyone did, he was never satisfied. But I didn't let my anger out. I didn't know how to. So I continued serving him, catering to his needs, and my anger remained stagnant inside of me.

Tuesday, January 12

It happened more than eight weeks ago.

It happened yesterday.

It happened an hour ago.

Time feels so arbitrary and so misleading. What is it, anyway? A way to count toward something, or away from something? I want to count away from my dad's death, but I can't. It feels like it could have happened so recently. When I feel those strong emotions, like it has just happened, I feel guilty for feeling them. It's been over eight weeks, and I am still so weak and volatile.

Time means nothing to me anymore. A week can pass in the blink of an eye, and a day can pass in what feels like a lifetime. I can feel an hour's worth of emotions in one minute, or go a day without feeling anything. It's scary and twisted. I can't control it, yet I feel like someone is controlling it. I just don't know who.

What do you think?

Have you ever been in a situation in which you felt like you didn't have any control? Write about or draw a sketch of the situation and your emotions surrounding it.

Tuesday, January 19

My thoughts are my worst enemy, a venom I can't control. Sometimes I don't even realize that I'm thinking about my dad until I start to feel very empty and alone.

It's been more than two months, and I still feel so emotionally unstable. Anything, even the tiniest little reminder of my dad can just set my mood off. Or, I can be in an excellent mood and then feel guilty about it. I think, 'How can I be enjoying myself when Dad was so unhappy that he killed himself?' These thoughts are the things that drive me crazy, but I don't know how to stop them.

> Darkness
> haunts my mind, my body
> grasps on tight
> so I can't let it go
> deep and brooding
> thoughts are inescapable
> this is me
>
> No, I want it to stop
> but I can't make it
> it has overtaken me
> my mind is my keeper
> I am just a shadow
> in the darkness

Thursday, January 28

We're reading "Jane Eyre" in English class. Today, my teacher said, "And how does John Reed die?" and everyone chimed, "Suicide!" Whenever I hear the word suicide it cuts me like a sharp knife. That was an unexpected blow and I felt dizzy. It's weird how even so long after he died, one word can affect me so greatly.

People keep asking me how I'm doing, and every time I say "good" and fake a smile I fall deeper into a hole. It's so hard. Sometimes my real emotions just spill out when I'm least expecting them to. I let out my anger on the wrong people. I don't know how I'm supposed to deal with these heavy feelings. I've never felt this way before and it's scary. I'm even scared of myself.

I thought a lot today about a night a few months ago when my dad was yelling at me a lot. I couldn't take it, and just went out onto the fire escape and sat there for an hour. My mom let me know when my dad went back upstairs. I feel like that all the time now. I don't know what to do or where to go, so my response is to just separate myself from the situation. I know this is just a temporary solution, but it helps to take a minute away from other people to be alone and stabilize my thoughts.

What do you think?

Sometimes there is no immediate solution to a problem. There's no need to handle everything all at once, so taking a break every now and then is a good way to stay calm and keep your emotions in check. Where can you go to feel safe and to get calm and centered?

Thursday, February 4

Last night I had a dream that my cat died. I was bawling and extremely emotional, and my mom remained cold and stern. She calmly buried him and I couldn't control myself. It reminds me of how I feel now: I have these intense, raging emotions inside me that I can hardly grasp, and my mom is going on with her life as usual. We only talk about Dad when I bring him up.

There are so many things I want to say to my dad. I got a 100 on my French test! I finally learned all the presidents! I'm visiting my sister Rebecca at college in a week, I'm getting a haircut soon, I'm getting an X-ray next week, I just cured cancer, I won the lottery, I'm flying to the moon, I'm sailing to the stars, I'm drifting away.

But I can't tell him anything, not anymore, not ever.

What do you think?

Do you have something you would like to say to the person you lost?

Saturday, February 13

Last night I had my first dream in which my dad was dead. He had been dead for three months, and my mom was pregnant. I kept saying to her how dangerous it was for her to be pregnant at her age but she was insisting on having the baby.

I had a pretty bad week. On Thursday morning, I went to the back doctor and found out that I most likely have a fracture in my lower back. I might have to wear a back brace and not play on the tennis team, which I did last year and have been looking forward to all year. The creepy part is my dad also had back problems, which started being a big problem when he was 15 years old.

My mom and dad met playing tennis. My mom was playing with her friend Lynn and my dad was playing with his friend Jim. It had rained the day before, and the courts were wet. My dad offered my mom the squeegee to dry off her court, and she asked him if he and Jim wanted to play with her and Lynn. They played, and after that they set up a date to play again. They soon fell in love and moved in together.

The most frustrating thing is that my mom sort of knew what she was getting in to. She knew my dad had depression and easily lost his temper. One time, when they had been dating for about a year, she simply asked him what he wanted for dinner and he totally lost it. She left the apartment and a few hours later, came back to find him lying in bed. Then he started talking about what a difficult person he was and that she'd probably want to leave him. But no, she stayed with him, and went into therapy to solve her problems. She didn't see the danger and thought she could fix him.

But you can't fix someone as messed up as my dad was. Any parent who puts himself and his needs before everyone else, even his kids, is really messed up. Any parent who feels justified in screaming at his child and insulting her, verbally abusing her, is seriously troubled. Why couldn't my mom see that?

Maybe she knew it all, deep down, but didn't want to see it. And after tons of therapy, she finally came to terms with it. She finally expressed her unhappiness with the marriage and told him she might not be able to go on with it. She finally would consider claiming her and my independence from the monster that had been ruining our lives.

He retaliated. He retaliated in the most angry, ferocious, selfish way possible -- suicide. That is the most destructive way to die. In a figurative sense, he had to have the last laugh.

In a literal sense, he had to prove to my mom that he "couldn't" go on without her.

In my opinion, he had to do the meanest, most horrible, most brutal thing he could do, the thing that could inflict the most pain on everyone around him that he wasn't man enough to deal with himself.

Wednesday, February 17

I'm visiting my sister at college right now. It's pretty fun and it's a nice distraction. I thought yesterday would be difficult because it was three months since my dad died, but it wasn't because I was so busy. All the kids on Rebecca's floor know about my dad. It's almost like I don't want them, or anyone, to know. Then maybe I can act like myself. But since everyone knows, I feel like they want me to be a certain way, which I can't be.

I want to go somewhere where no one knows me or my back story. I want to be anonymous and be able to start from scratch. Or even better, I could be a different person with a normal family, and I wouldn't care if people knew about my life or not. Because it would be normal. Accepted. Common.

I wouldn't be an outcast like I am now. I wouldn't have to go through twenty emotions a minute or worry about everything I say and do or try to suppress my tears when I hear something about suicide.

The only place I'm free to express myself now is in my mind. I'm scared to do even that though, because then I dream about what I'm thinking. Dreams are so frightening and always contain the most wretched, horrifying thing I thought of in the entire day. It's like someone is looking at a pool of my thoughts and picking the worst ones to put in my dreams. Even when I've had a great day and hardly thought about Dad, I dream about him.

My therapist says, "It's only a dream, it can't hurt you." But it's more than a dream. It's my life and my reality; it's inescapable; an inconvenient truth.

Wednesday, February 24

I've been doing okay this week. It's gone by pretty quickly so far and I haven't thought about my dad too much. The only major thing that happened was that on Tuesday in History, my teacher was telling us about taking AP courses next year, and she said "don't kill yourselves with work," and I felt a little jolt. She called me over after class and apologized, which I thought was really sweet. She and my English teacher are the only teachers who know how my dad died.

My mom is pretty much the only person I talk about Dad to. I suppose I could confide in Kayla or some other good friend. But it just feels so weird. I feel like my thoughts and emotions are mine, and no one else's. Why should they know what I'm thinking? And even if I did see a reason in telling them, wouldn't it just burden them to know what I'm brooding over? Why would they want to waste their time trying to analyze my strange thoughts when I can't even comprehend them myself?

That's probably not true, but that's the way it feels. I am so bothered by my own thoughts that I know no one else would want to hear them either. Sometimes they swell up inside me, and I feel like I need to say them to someone, but I don't.

the fire burns within me
the flame flickers bright
emotions swirl round in a cauldron
revolving, spinning, tossing, turning
flashing light throughout

the fire burns within me
it catches things aflame
I burn them out with my breath
but they remain charred
scarred
imprinted

the fire burns within me
I can't put it out
it grows and shrinks
always at the least a tiny flame
burning brightly
inside me

What do you think?

Although I had trouble talking to my friends, sometimes it feels like it might be easier to tell a stranger our most personal thoughts and feelings than a best friend. We value our friends' opinions so much, and we don't want them to judge us, so sometimes we don't even tell them about huge issues in our lives. For a while I avoided talking to my friends about my dad and instead kept my feelings to myself. I realize now that they wouldn't have judged me, and that they were all on my side. Opening up to people is still a big challenge for me, but my close friends have all been so loving and supportive that I now realize how important and therapeutic it is to talk about difficult issues with them. Even though it might be difficult, with whom might you share your deepest feelings?

Saturday, March 6

I think I went a whole three hours without thinking about my dad today. I was baking cookies and singing songs and couldn't focus on anything else but the task at hand. When I was done and I realized that I hadn't thought about him for so long, the first thing I felt was a pang of guilt. Then I got mad at myself for feeling that. But I couldn't help it. I feel like I should be thinking about him constantly. I feel like he deserves it in some weird way.

I really do miss my dad. That's the most confusing, messed up thing, because he was so mean to me. He made me feel bad about myself whenever I was around him. He didn't care about me or my feelings. But sometimes he was nice, and that's what I miss. My mom says she sometimes feels lonely, and she thinks she misses Dad, but she really misses the old Dad. Before he quit his real job and started playing poker, before his addiction, before his depression and behavior got out of hand, before, before ...

What do you think?

What are some good memories you have of the person you lost?

Wednesday, March 10

I am a soldier, armed and ready.
I am a mountain, tall and sturdy.
I am a rock, cold and hard.
I am a volcano, furious and unpredictable.
I am a child, alone and scared.

I am about ready to explode. I didn't think I was much of an actress before, but now I'm acting every day. I act every time someone says anything that makes me think of my dad. I act like I'm okay and that I didn't even notice what they said. The truth is, I heard it loud and clear like someone was shouting it in my ear. I heard it louder and many more times than everyone else.

Everything leaves an impression on me. I replay conversations, phrases, and words that bothered me when I first heard them. I try to analyze my feelings and reactions but my mind just wanders onto something else and I lose focus.

I feel so out of it. I can't really focus on anything. Whenever a part of me wants to try to let go of what happened, the other part pulls me back. It's like a tug of war is going on inside my head.

Wednesday, March 17

My dad hung himself in a closet.

My dear father passed away on November 16th, 2009.

Dad tied a belt around his neck and hung from the bar in his closet.

My daddy died at home.

My dad is a selfish jerk who took his own life to make a statement.

Daddy had some problems and was very confused.

What's right? What's wrong? What's the truth and what is a lie? There are so many questions that can never be answered. These are the things that haunt me: the unanswerable, the unimaginable, the unthinkable. This is why I hate the quiet and the noise. The light and the dark. The alive and the dead.

But mostly the dead.

Sunday, March 21

I wanted to pop a few weeks ago when my mom told me she had been talking with a guy at her sports club and wanted to take her wedding ring off. "What are you doing? Your husband died four months ago and now you're self-conscious about your wedding ring when you're talking with a total stranger?"

I want to pop right now and release everything inside of me. I want to break the hard shell separating me from the rest of the world. I want to understand why I think the things I think and feel the way I feel.

What do you think?

I struggled a lot with acknowledging my feelings and letting out my emotions during this time. Instead of tucking them in a corner, it's important to recognize your feelings so you can try to understand them better. Draw a picture of yourself and all the issues weighing down on your mind right now, and brainstorm a few things you can do to lighten the load, whether it be exercising, writing, talking to a friend, or something else.

Thursday, March 25

The funeral is the weirdest thing. The first funeral I ever went to was my own father's. The whole thing felt unreal and even when I spoke I wasn't really there. The hugs, the tears, the prayers; all of it just felt like it was a mile away from me. I was living in the past, in my not-so-happy but not-horrible past. I didn't have a dead father. Maybe my sister did, but not me. Because it couldn't have actually happened. This thing doesn't really happen. You hear about it, but it doesn't happen to you.

Apparently it happened to me though, and I still don't believe it. I still want to talk to my dad. I want to go back, but I also don't. Is my life better without him, or worse? Will I be overall happier or sadder?

Last night I had a dream where my dad came back from the dead. He had killed himself, but then he came back. In my dream I was really upset, and I wanted him to be dead, but when I woke up I felt bad about feeling that. How could I want him to be dead? My dad is a part of me. Everything that he did had an impact on me. And so did his death. I just don't want that to be a part of me. But it is, and I can't deny it.

What do you think?

What is something that you regret having happened, and how can you accept it as part of your life?

Saturday, March 27

I remember the night it happened so vividly. My mom and I entered the house and only one light was on. As we walked up the stairs I saw a sticky note on my dad's computer. I took the note and tried to read it, but the only thing I saw was "suicide note." I later found out that the note had instructions to finding the suicide note on my dad's computer.

My mom told me to stay where I was and went upstairs. I stood by the stairs, leaning against the banister, confused. I don't think I had yet processed the fact that he could be dead. But when my mom came downstairs and shakily said, "I need to call 9-1-1" it clicked.

I dropped down to the kitchen floor and went ballistic. I cried and screamed so loud that my mom couldn't hear the dispatcher on the phone and had to go onto the porch. I don't know if I was even thinking, I was crying so hard.

Everything happened so fast after that. The police and ambulance arrived. They went up to my parents' room and confirmed that my dad was dead. Meanwhile, Mom and I sat in the family room and she attempted to call her family to tell them what happened, but no one would answer their phone. She reached Ahava, Kayla's mom. Ahava came to pick me up and bring me to her house so I wouldn't have to see the body being brought downstairs. I shakily walked to her car and thought I would faint. I felt limp like a piece of spaghetti. I couldn't see clearly or hear anything she was saying to me. In the car I kept crying and feeling helpless and wary.

When we drove up to Kayla's house, I saw her standing at the window in her room. When she saw the car, she let the shade drop and came downstairs. I fell into her arms.

Kayla and I went to her room and sat on her bed and cried. I cried because I couldn't be with my mom. I wanted to be near her so badly. Kayla and I lay down, then sat up, then went downstairs and watched "Spongebob." Kayla thought it would help me think about something else for a little bit, and she was right. I ceased crying and focused intently on the television screen. When the show ended, my life resumed.

I called my mom and I still couldn't go back home. Kayla and I sat in her living room and my crying let up a bit. Finally I was allowed to go home. My mom and I hugged and sat together while streams of people, friends and strangers, swarmed into and out of our house. When they all left around midnight, Mom and I lay down on the couch in the family room and tried to go to sleep. This being unsuccessful, we sat up again and cried some more. Her sisters and mother, having finally received her call, arrived at about 1:00 A.M. We sat up with them for an hour or so, and then everyone went to bed. I actually slept. I slept for six whole hours. My mom couldn't sleep because my sister still didn't know. She said the day wasn't complete until Rebecca knew.

The following morning, Mom called Rebecca's college and asked to speak to the dean. The dean went to Rebecca's room and sat with her as my mom broke the news to her. Rebecca cried, but pulled it together when she had to pack. She was strong and steady throughout her whole trip home, and only cracked once she was in the privacy of our home. I'll always admire the courage it must have taken her to stay calm and level-headed that whole day.

What do you think?

Have you ever had to stay calm and level-headed through a crisis?

Friday, April 9

Around the time of the intervention, my dad and my mom fought a ton. I remember one night I was trying to go to sleep and all I could hear was them yelling at each other. I came out of my room and sat at the top of the stairs. I heard my mom crying and my dad yelling at her, "You chose to stay married to me! You wanted this! You chose to put up with me!"

That's when the fear really started building. After that night I realized the true wrath of my dad and tried to avoid him as much as possible. That was only worse for me, though. He'd get mad at me for not being loving enough and not talking to him enough.

There was always something or someone to be blamed for my dad's behavior. It was never his fault. It was his body pain, it was the medicine, it was his mother, etcetera. Around the time of the intervention it was his medicine. He blamed all of his crazy behaviors, like raiding the kitchen for food in the middle of the night and leaving it a complete mess, on the medicine. After the medicine, he blamed his behavior on his mother. She wanted to tear him apart and ruin his life. He was so delusional. He could live in his own little world, completely disconnected from reality. Whatever happened between him and his mother, she didn't cause his behavior. He was a grown man and he could make his own decisions. Instead, he acted horribly and pinned the blame on her, trying to make my sister and me think that she was the bad one, not him.

Last, he blamed me. He wasn't receiving the amount of love and affection he wanted from my mom, so he expected it from me. When I didn't provide that, he lashed out. He said awful things to me and made me feel horrible about myself. I didn't want to even look at him, but since my mom was working so much, I was forced to. I had to suffer through his self-centered speeches, ridiculous arguments, and harsh words every single day. And my mom didn't intervene.

My dad found a way to have the last say. Like he always did. He had to be the center of attention in any way possible.

Looks like he got what he asked for.

What do you think?

It was really difficult for me to come home from school every day and have to deal with my dad. It took me a long time after he died to realize that he had been verbally abusing me. If I had spoken up and told a friend or adult about what was going on at home, I might have been able to recognize this sooner and deal with it head-on. Don't be afraid to speak up if you don't feel comfortable or safe at home, at school, or anywhere; telling somebody will help you gain clarity about the situation.

Who would you be comfortable talking to? What would it be like to tell him or her?

Thursday, April 15

Today is my dad's birthday. I was determined not to be upset but I was. I was in a funk at school and couldn't focus on anything. I kept picturing my dad and wanting to tell him things. I tried to isolate myself from everyone but it didn't work. My mood went up and down really quickly; I'd feel like the weight was lifting off my shoulders one minute, and the next I'd be back into my state of stillness and darkness. My mood was lifted permanently after school though, when my tennis coach told me I was going to play varsity that day. My first varsity match ever. The bad thoughts about my dad flew out of my head and I played my hardest. My partner and I won 6-2, 6-1. I'm proud of myself for being able to let go when I had to; it's nice knowing that there's something I can do to take my mind off my dad.

What do you think?

In addition to writing, playing tennis is a way I can escape from pressures in my life. Whenever I'm dealing with anything difficult or stressful, going out and hitting a few tennis balls makes me feel a lot better. What are your three favorite activities to do that put you in a good mood and take your mind off things? Write about how you feel when you're doing these activities.

Friday, April 23

My dad had a lot of trouble getting along with my mom's family. I admit they aren't the easiest people to get along with. But no one is. Everyone has their faults, and part of having a relationship with any person is working around those faults and trying to get along. My dad would have none of that. If things weren't exactly the way he wanted, he sulked like a little kid and complained. He had so many faults but if anyone else had a fault he couldn't compromise.

One time my mom, dad, sister, and I were driving home from a family gathering. My dad was sitting in the passenger seat with his trademark gloomy stare on his face. The rest of us were being quiet, because we knew that anything we said would set him off. We drove by a gas station, and my dad said to my mom, "Why don't you just leave me here." He was completely serious. He was such a drama queen that he told my mom in front of my sister and me to leave him at the gas station! He said that that's how my mom's family made him feel. My parents got in a huge argument. I burst into tears, and my mom tried to calm things down but my dad continued yelling. He didn't care how I felt. He wanted to scream, so he screamed. No one else had a say. My mom was too scared, my sister was too scared, and I was too scared. He had complete control. It felt as if he were standing in front of me spitting in my face and there was nothing I could do about it.

I never felt so powerless as when my dad was angry. He was a monster. My mom, sister, and I were innocent little bugs he stepped on. All the tears meant nothing. All the words meant nothing. All that mattered was my dad and his big, fat emotions that could take up a whole room and suffocate everyone in it.

He made me feel so horrible. He made me hate myself.

Don't hurt me. Please, just leave me alone.

Sunday, May 2

people talk about you
like a monster
like an evil foe who took away my and my
mom's freedom
like a beast
it's easy to blame the one who can't defend
himself, isn't it

we think
we're better than you
we think you didn't deserve us
we think we're better off now
without you

would you be ashamed?
would you be angry, frustrated?
standing there, arms crossed, watching us
shaking your head in disapproval
not speaking

we don't need to know
we don't want to know
I think it will be easier for me,
for my mom,

if we just shut you out
let's do it

let's remove this from our lives
from our minds, our bodies
let's live freely and serenely
nothing can stop us now, no
nothing is in our way

life in all its glory before me
what ever shall I do with it?

Friday, May 21

I sprained my ankle yesterday. My mom had to come home from a long day of work and instead of getting to go home, eat some dinner, and relax, she had to take me to the ER where we spent almost three hours. I felt horrible for her but there was nothing I could do. I wanted my dad to be there, strangely enough. The very few times he was kind to me were when I was hurt. I cherished those times and long for them all the time. My dad should have been there. He would have been there. Don't parents want to be there when their kids are hurt? Isn't that their job? Did it occur to him that when he killed himself he would also be leaving a hole in my life?

> I want to know what he was thinking
> I want to know what one could be thinking
> right before tying the belt
> around his neck
>
> I want to know why
> he would do something irreversible like that
> no second chances
> what's done is done

I want to know if
he thought of me at all
if my image, or words, or anything
even graced his burning thoughts

I don't think so
I think all that he was thinking about
then,
all that he was thinking about ever,
all that he was even capable of thinking
about,
was himself.

Sunday, May 23

People are still asking me how I'm doing. I find that it's easier to say "fine" now than it used to be. What hasn't gotten any easier is when people sit there talking about suicide, with their misconceptions and judgments, and I have to listen to them.

I don't know why, but thinking about arriving at Kayla's house makes me the most emotional. Maybe it was her dad hugging me, maybe it was her level-headedness, maybe it was the fact that going to her house didn't feel to me like I was leaving home at all, but rather going home. Maybe because her family feels like my family. They lost my dad just as much as I did. Their pain was just as great as mine, and, even though unspoken, it was known.

It's the little things that get to me the most. The little nods, gestures, unspoken agreements. The feeling of closeness and security. The opposite of what I felt whenever I was around my dad.

What do you think?

Sometimes people can mean more to us than we ever would have imagined. When I was dealing with the worst of my dad, Kayla's house was my refuge. If things are rough at home, having a place where you feel completely safe outside of your house can be a huge help.

Where is your safe place—your "house of refuge"?

Wednesday, June 2

There's less than a month of school left, and I can't believe it. It feels like the year just flew by. It's weird though, because seeing what has happened this year it would seem like it would have felt really slow. I think it did feel slow while I was going through it, but now it's all a blur. It happened, I was sad, and now I'm ... happy?

I don't know what I am. I'm generally in a good mood during school, with friends, classes, and everything. And then after school I go to tennis, and that makes me happy. The only time I'm sad is when I'm alone with my thoughts. Otherwise I'm too busy to even notice them.

But those times, when it's just me and them, can get really bad. Nothing is there to stop me or distract me, and my thoughts can wind and twist in any dark way they want to. Sometimes I don't even realize what I'm thinking until I feel my mood sinking. I find that now though, it's easier to pull myself out than it used to be. A little TV, a phone call with a friend, anything can brighten my mood back up again. Because I have so many good things in my life, and I'm finally ready to let them back in.

What do you think?

What are some good things you can let back into your life?

Tuesday, June 8

If you want to judge me, go right ahead.
You can stick a label on my forehead.
You can say whatever you want right to my
face.
It won't faze me.

If you want to stare at me, be my guest.
I'll just stare right back.
You can laugh, you can cry.
You can try to understand, or you can try to
forget.
It won't matter to me.

I'm sick of thinking about what you want.
I'm done caring about what you think.
I'm ready to think about me, mine, my.
Yours just doesn't ring so clearly, so freely.

I'd rather be myself, thank you.
I'd rather not have to worry about you.
So I'm just going to do whatever I'd like.
And you and yours can watch me.

Friday, June 11

He was supposed to remember.

The one thing I asked him to remember. I made him promise over and over. His job was to remember that I wanted to have French onion soup at my wedding. If there was one thing he'd ever do for me, it was to remember that.

It seems so insignificant. Why does remembering French onion soup matter so much? It's just that that was the one thing I really counted on him for, something solid. It was our thing, something I thought I'd be able to share with him forever. And then on my wedding day, he could walk me down the aisle, happy, smiling, his youngest daughter starting her happy-ever-after life.

It makes me so mad. I had no control over this event that hit me like a tidal wave. If I knew, I might have at least worn a life vest. But I wasn't prepared -- no one was. And now we all have to try to move on as if the tidal wave never washed over us, never took our breath away and made us feel like we were drowning. We have to be expert swimmers who can help other people who might not be so steady.

I was looking at my mom's "Mother's Memories" book, and I saw something she had written about my sister when she was four. My sister had drawn my dad a picture and told him to keep it forever and ever, and when he was ready to die he could throw it out. Was he ready to die? If he even remembered, would he have thrown out the picture?

What makes someone ready to die? Does he have to accomplish his life goals, be a true Renaissance man, have a loving family, what? Or does it mean just being able to anticipate death? In that case, my dad was ready.

I don't think he was ready, though. He just felt that it was his only option. For me, being ready for death would mean living life to its fullest all the way through and not taking anything for granted. I'm going to try to deviate from my dad's way of living and follow my own advice, but it might be hard.

What do you think?

What does "Living life to the fullest" mean to you?

Sunday, June 20

It's Father's Day today, and it was my parents' anniversary yesterday. I was fine yesterday but my mom wasn't. Today I feel worse than I've felt in months.

I don't wish my dad were here, I just wish it weren't Father's Day. I'm jealous of all of the families I saw out and about today, and I'm jealous of all the handsome dads in the Father's Day ads, which seem to be everywhere I look. I can make myself look away, but the damage has been dealt.

I can't smile and I can't be in a good mood. Not crying or screaming takes up all the energy I have. I need to be in my own world, away from the insensitivities and cruelty of the uncaring, unfeeling world around me.

But that's not even the problem. The world is plenty kind and feeling. Maybe it's just me, then. I just can't fit in to this welcoming world and I am an outcast.

Now I'm crying and I can't stop. Why can't I have any control over myself or my own life?

What do you think?

Father's Day was particularly difficult for me because it felt like I was being forced to focus on my dad, and all the emotions that I thought I was done experiencing came back. I was mad at myself for feeling that way again, which made it even worse. I know now though that it's okay to feel that way every once in a while; even now, I still have days like that. But I feel that way less and less often, and when the feelings do resurface, I use one of my escape methods to cope with them and I feel back to normal soon after.

Do you feel yourself going through ups and downs, too? What is this like for you?

Thursday, June 24

I haven't thought about Dad too much this week, not counting Father's Day. I've been busy baby-sitting and haven't really had time. I guess that's what my mom and grandma keep talking about; keeping themselves busy stops them from thinking about him. That works pretty well for me too.

My mom made an account on a dating web site. That made me feel pretty bad. How could I even comprehend accepting a new man into our lives? I want my mom to myself. Just because she's willing to let a complete stranger into our lives doesn't mean I am.

And of course, I started thinking about the future; she could get married again. I could have stepsiblings. That thought is so alien, and I barely even understand it. How can new people be dumped into my life like that? I shy away from these thoughts and don't want to have any part in them. I just hope my mom doesn't go that far, or at least not soon. I can barely handle everything going on now, and I can only imagine what life would be like with a new, fake family.

Sunday, June 27

I have a friend whose parents are divorced and her mom is now dating online, and she is in a similar situation as I am. She said that I should give my mom an opportunity to tell me about her dating life. I was planning on doing so, but then at dinner my sister asked "So, any progress with the online dating?" My mom replied, "I'll let you know when there's something I'm willing to share." Now I feel bad that I know about her little "dating secret," but I'm also angry at her for not telling me. We tell each other everything. We're closer than any other friend of mine is with her mom. So why not tell me this? Maybe because she knows I don't want her to be dating.

Doesn't that sound wrong? My mom isn't telling me about her love life because she thinks I'll disapprove. It feels like a bit of role reversal; she's like the young, rebellious teen, while I'm the conservative mother. Whatever it is, I don't like it and I don't want my mom to be doing this behind my back. It's hard enough to accept the fact that she's dating in the first place, and the whole secrecy element just adds to my discomfort.

are you there?

can you hear me?

I want you to tell me

what is going on

are you there?
do you see me?
or am I just slowly,
slowly fading away

are you there?
do you need me?
are we close,
or drifting farther
and farther
apart?

Wednesday, July 7

I was just thinking about my eulogy and how angry and ferocious it was. Only two days after Dad died I was able to directly express all my frustration with him in sharp, piercing words, and the next day was able to deliver those words to more than 100 people. The depth of my emotions and fierce hate of my dad scares me. Even right after he died the cruelest, most awful feelings I had toward him poured out of me like they had been waiting to for so long. It's overwhelming but relieving at the same time. My ability to express my feelings can be viewed as a positive thing, but their intensity might not be so good.

I guess my feelings seemed so intense after my dad died because they weren't just feelings about his death. They were feelings of hurt, anger, fear, and untapped angst built up from the past few years, finally able to escape. Before I had been too scared to let my feelings out, but after my dad died and still now, I let them fly freely.

> your words
> leave a mark on me
> I can hide it, I can hide it all right
> but it's still there

it's there, gaining strength
revolving wildly, mustering up courage
I can wait, I can wait for you
are you ready for me?

I feel my body surging with energy
your words have lit a fuse, and it's
dancing, I'm dancing around
do you catch my beat?

I stop, stand still
you're no longer there
my body stops whirring, the mark
stops pulsing, I am calm, I am serene
I am me, I
am free.

What do you think?

I surprised myself with the intensity of emotion I felt after my dad's death. Have you ever been surprised by your own emotions, like reacting in a way you didn't think you would to something that happened? Write about it or sketch a picture depicting the situation.

Friday, July 16

It was my birthday two days ago, and I really had an amazing day. Nothing, not even those pathetic, creepy thoughts, stopped me from having a wonderful time and enjoying everything to the fullest. I felt so great and relaxed and mature and just plain happy. The only time I found myself missing my dad was when I got my permit. I had been planning to take the permit test on my birthday for months and months, and had prepared extremely hard for it. I was surprised to find how easy the test was and told all my friends about it, but I would have loved to see the look on his face when I broke the news to him.

I might have done it jokingly, as I often did when I got a good grade on a test or something of the sort. I'd enter the room and he'd be sitting on the couch, reading something. I'd carefully walk over to him, a solemn, worried look hiding a huge grin underneath. "Dad," I'd say. "Yes?" He'd ask, looking up from his reading material. "You know that permit test, right?" "Yes." "Well ... I didn't exactly do as well as I thought." He'd raise his eyebrows, but then think I was joking. "Sure, Ilana," he'd say, with only a hint of worry in his voice. I'd give a stern look and repeat myself, and let him know that I didn't pass the test. By this point he'd surely believe me, and start telling me about how I should have studied harder, or not have taken the test on my birthday, or something, while a big smile spread across my face.

Then he'd realize that I'd tricked him like I always did, and that he'd fallen for it like he always did. He'd give me a look, but then laugh and say, "You're a nutball," or one of his other endearing terms. I'd smile with pride and go on to tell him how easy the test was.

What do you think?

Looking back, I'm proud of myself for not letting my desire to gloat to my dad stop me from being in a good mood. If it were a few months earlier, something like that might have ruined the rest of my day. But now I'm more capable of detaching myself from those kinds of thoughts and feelings and just continuing forward. I'm glad I've been able to acquire this skill, and I hope that I will continue to be able to use it.

When have you noticed that you've been able to detach yourself from a situation that potentially might cause you to feel badly? Write about or draw a picture of that time.

Thursday, July 22

I was cleaning out my closet, and I found the following letter:

Sept. 17, 2008

Dear Ilana,

Mommy told me how upset you were last night. I was completely shocked as I was not even feeling mad at you.

I am very sorry that I did anything to make you feel so bad. I love you with all my heart and never want to hurt you in any way. I know that when I get a little frustrated or mad at you it can seem that I am more frustrated or mad than I really am. I think it's because I care so much about you being a good person. And then if we add in your extra sensitivity, what started out as a little thing ends up seeming much bigger than it really is.

Please try to always remember that I love you enormously even when I behave in a way that upsets you.

Love,

Daddy

I don't even remember what happened to make him write this letter. I don't distinguish one event from another in my mind of him yelling at me, insulting me, or anything. It's all just a blurry bunch of thoughts swarming around. But this letter makes me want to forgive him for everything. It is so nice and kind and it makes me want to give him a hug, and let everything go, and be happy and loved. It makes me believe that he really did love me and he always wanted to do things in my better interest.

But then I think of what happened. If any of what he wrote in this letter is true, how could he have killed himself? He said he never wanted to hurt me in any way. Did he think killing himself wouldn't hurt me?

I try to block it out and just think about how "sick" he was. I don't want it to have anything to do with me. But reading this letter made me miss him so much, despite everything that happened.

The emotions expressed in the letter can't be faked; I know he loved me. I know he cared. And that's why it's so difficult for me to understand what happened. It's like there's a piece missing, something that could explain the reasoning behind what he did. But he's not here to explain it to me. All he did was leave me with this emptiness I am blindly wandering in, trying to make sense of, while knowing it is totally nonsensical.

Tuesday, August 3

I think that I've thought more than every single thought in the world combined. I think so much that my mind seems to have adapted to a constant rhythm of whirring around in orderly chaos. One thought outweighs another, then sits beside another, then leaps toward another, which brings me back to the first. I've exhausted every possibility, movement, utterance of speech, hint, time, anything I can wrap my brain around.

What am I thinking about? I'm thinking about my friends, school, my mom and sister, the summer, and most of all, but less and less so, my dad. It's not the heavy, pressuring thoughts it used to be that would weigh me down and take me out with one punch. It's more like ideas, stories, and interpretations. What happened. What didn't happen. What could've, should've, just might've happened, if only.

Although there is and always will be a void of unanswerable questions, I'm becoming more content with it. Instead of distressing over words not spoken, thoughts not shared, I try to focus on the definite words and thoughts I can grasp. I don't know everything about the situation, and I never will, but like Simon and Garfunkel said, it's "like emptiness in harmony." I'm learning to be okay with the unknown, and moving on with my life despite it.

What do you think?

Here, I am finally beginning to come to terms with the fact that I will never know all the details about my dad's death. This was a big step for me, and took a very long time because I had so many unanswered questions. Sometimes you just have to accept what's given to you and let go, even if it is difficult to do, so that you can move on.

What are you ready to accept?

Tuesday, August 17

    I remember one afternoon specifically as being the worst day ever with my dad. I came home from school and walked up the stairs, yelling "Hi" to my dad as I came in. He was sitting in the family room. As I put my backpack down and started to get my homework out, he loudly said to me, "Aren't you even going to say hello to me?" I was a little confused, dropped what I was doing, and poked my head into the room to say hi again. He glared at me and said, "You're not even going to show me your face?" I must have looked perplexed because he became angrier and screamed at me, "You are so rude to me! You make me feel horrible! All I ask for is a simple hello and you don't even care! I sit here all day alone and all I want is a hello from my daughter!" I started to shrink as he shouted at me, and I could feel tears start to sting my eyes. I managed a "sorry," went upstairs to my room, and locked the door. I sat on my bed and tried to cry softly so he wouldn't hear. A few minutes later he came up and banged on my door. I didn't answer and pleaded that he just leave me alone. He continued banging and started yelling at me, "Open the door! You can't lock me out of here! I'll take the hinges off the door!" I was worried he was going to hit me or something so I didn't open the door. He said, "I can't believe you're acting like I did something to you! You did this to me, Ilana! Let me in!" I finally got up and opened the door. I got back into my bed and silently pulled the covers around my body. He sat on the edge of my bed and lectured me for 45 whole minutes about how horrible I am to him, how terrible his life is, and how I should show him some respect. He kept asking me questions, and I wouldn't answer, I couldn't answer, and he started yelling again, "Answer me! Answer me!" I was so scared that I began to tremble. He leaned in closer, got up and walked right over to me and brought his face inches away from mine, so that with every word he spoke I felt his spit hitting my face. I flinched, and he got angrier, screaming louder, "Answer me god dammit!" I felt like I was going to die, or at least I'd rather have died than endure this pain. Finally, after what felt like hours he left my room and went back to his cave. I ran out, not knowing where to go, dazed and confused and dizzy. I thought about going to Kayla's house but she wasn't home. I had absolutely nowhere to go and all I knew was that I couldn't go back to the house. I went and sat on the fire escape outside the kitchen. After an hour of sitting there in the cold I decided to peek inside to see if my dad was there. He was not in sight, so I quickly went to the kitchen to get some dinner, when he appeared at the doorway. He tried to talk to me, he reached out to grab my arm, but I pulled away and escaped to my room again. I refused to come out, and wouldn't open the door until my mom came home. I explained everything to her, bursting out in tears.

That was the scariest day of my life. I felt physically threatened by my dad. And that was the final straw for my mom realizing things couldn't go on as they were. So maybe it's my fault my dad died. But maybe it's not. He did this to me, I didn't do it to him. He did it to himself. It's not my fault, no matter how many times he told me it was. Now I just have to believe it.

What do you think?

Clearly, this day was the most painful day I had to go through when my dad was still alive. I can't change the way that things happened on that day, but I can use the memory of it to remind myself that I wasn't doing anything wrong.

Do you have any memories that are difficult to think about, but hold a deep significance for you?

Saturday, August 21

I feel so much freer than I used to. Before, when my dad was in chronic pain, whenever he couldn't do something active with the rest of the family, he'd get mad at us. Instead of being happy that we could go do something fun, he'd guilt trip us for doing it. Last year, my mom and I decided we were going to do the whole Walk for Hunger, which is 20 miles. We were so pumped and were having fun doing it. Then, after 10 miles, my dad called my mom and told us to come home. It was like my mom was a puppet and he controlled her strings. We had been planning to do the whole walk, we were doing really well and then poof, my dad flipped the switch and we had to go home. He made us feel horrible for doing the walk in the first place and leaving him alone at home. I was so mad at my mom for obeying him. I wanted to keep walking! Why did he get to decide what we did? Didn't my mom have a mind of her own? I protested and fought as much as I could but ultimately I had to take one of the buses home with my mom for people who give up in the middle of the walk. I couldn't have been angrier with her or my dad.

I don't get why she didn't take action. I guess she had fallen so deep into my dad's trap that she couldn't pull herself out. She had to do what he told her to, and resisting wasn't even an option. She had been doing it for so long that it felt natural for her.

You can get so immersed in another person sometimes that you lose yourself. He is a second part of you and you can't see anything clearly through your own eyes. That's what happened to my mom. But I know for sure that's never going to happen to me.

you may seem like a nice guy
to them
you can pull off anything
smart, funny, outgoing, gentle
artistic, altruistic, moralistic
they believe anything you tell them
but I see through that
I can see through your lies,
your fear, your pain, your desire
I see the real you
the person standing before me

through my eyes
you're not who you say you are
you're a fake, a liar, a phony
you just wish you were those things

you can't be who you wish you were
but you pretend
well stop pretending
it's not working
I know
who you are
and I don't like it

What do you think?

In what ways can you always stay true to yourself?

Monday, August 30

It's weird to think that I can barely remember the "good" dad my mom always talks about. According to her, he went "bad" when he quit his job at Lotus when I was six years old. I don't remember much before I was six. When I think really hard I can remember some tickle fights, and story times, and the way he used to brush my hair so gently that it didn't hurt. But most of those memories have almost completely faded, and I'm left to ponder the "bad" dad.

My sister can remember a lot more of the good dad than I can. I think there's a huge amount of cognitive development between the ages of six and nine. I wish I'd had those three extra years like she did. Why did I get the short end of the bargain? Why don't I get to have at least a few distant memories to grasp on to of my dad that might make me see him in a different way? All I have are photographs to remind me of what used to be, what could have been.

How can a person go from good to bad? How can someone not have enough contact with himself not to see that happening? How can someone go from a capable, thin, loving father and husband to a cruel, fat, ugly, heartless monster? I don't understand at all and thinking about it makes me so sad. A person was lost when my dad became what I remember of him. A normal person disappeared from the face of the earth, never to be seen again. That doesn't count as death though, does it? Losing yourself doesn't mean dying, as long as you're still walking and breathing. It's weird, because that seems like a more realistic form of death to me.

I'd rather be dead than lose myself. But was what my dad turned out to be in the end a completely different person than before? Or was that part of him there all along, just waiting for an opportunity to escape? It just seems so implausible that he could become something so drastically different from what he was before. Maybe bad dad is him. Maybe I knew him, I know him, I have known him all along. Maybe, just maybe, I didn't miss a thing.

Saturday, September 4

How many times do I have to say it for it to make sense? I feel like I've said it a million times, "My dad killed himself." Why does it still feel so fresh when I say it out loud? Besides saying those words, I feel like it happened so long ago, and that I've moved on so much. But just have me tell you what happened and it stings just as badly as it did the night it happened. I don't get why. Maybe it's because when I say it happened, I have to believe it, and I can't try to block it out. It's almost like I'm admitting it. Yes, this actually happened, there's no going back. When I'm just thinking about it in my head the thoughts aren't real, they're just my musings and imagination. Words solidify it. And it's that solid truth that scares me.

I just want to hug him. I want him to come back and be completely different. I would die for one more smile, laugh, anything. I miss him so much. Now I can separate in my mind the happy, fun dad from the cruel, evil one, and I can have different feelings toward them. I long for the fun dad. Thinking about hugging him makes me so happy but so sad, knowing that I'll never, ever have the chance to hug him again. Nothing, not double hugs from my mom, not pictures of my dad, nothing can fill that void. And nothing will ever be able to.

What helps is remembering the good times. The games, the jokes, the laughs. I feel warm inside when I remember my dad's bright, smiling eyes looking at me, lighting me up. I miss those days, but I also can remember the bad times and deep down I know that what happened was for the best, and that I can't go back to before. The past is over. Those distant memories will forever remain a part of me, but a part that I can't go back to.

What do you think?

In this entry, I finally decide that my dad's death happened for the best. It took months of thoughts, memories, and experiences to come to terms with that, but once I realized it, I felt a great wave of relief. Write about an experience in which you had to go through a long process to decide or declare something very important to you.

Tuesday, September 14

I'm starting to experience something I didn't think I would experience, at least not this soon. I'm starting to forget some things about him. I don't know how he would react in a certain situation, or what he'd say about something. I always used to be able to read him like a book; it wasn't hard because basically everything made him angry. But now I find myself wondering, 'Would he like this? Maybe this would change him ...'

The thought of him doesn't sicken me as much as it did before, because now it's not just an automatic association with screaming, yelling, and darkness. Those memories are still there, but now they're only slightly more prominent than the not-so-dark ones of years past. I think that's a good thing. I don't want to view him just as the person I knew him best as. People change. Even if they don't always change for the better, the person they used to be is still there somewhere. That is still a part of them, no matter how many layers of hurt, pain, and cruelty it's buried under. The thing I still don't understand is how a good person can let himself turn so bad, though. It's as if he had no sense of self, or self-understanding or anything. I know me, I know myself more than anyone else ever could. With my current level of sanity, how could I consciously turn into someone who I'd despise now? How could that just happen? Where did his self-awareness go?

Maybe he was just too self-centered and oblivious to realize what was happening. Even before he changed, he always thought he was right, and he was the best. Maybe as he started sliding down, he kept justifying his behaviors with selfish thoughts. No matter what he looked like or acted like, he was still Bennett the Great, the one above the rest. It's that superiority complex that did him in. If someone thinks the world revolves around him there's no way he's going to get by in life successfully. No one's going to stop in his path and worship him. He's just going to feel rejection after rejection, pain and more pain, until he sinks so far down that he's completely submerged, and feels that there's no way to get out.

Friday, October 1

Being back in school has made me start thinking about Dad a lot again. I think about how awful coming home from school in the fall last year was. Now, instead of coming home, I go to my friends' houses for dinner and my mom picks me up after. It's not ideal but it's better than eating alone. And it's better than eating with Dad. It's just that now that I'm in school I'm constantly reminded of the fact that I don't have a dad anymore, and it hurts. Why do all my friends get to have normal, functioning dads and I don't? What did I do wrong? It isn't fair.

In Spanish class we're reading a book called "La Dama Del Alba." I didn't really like it or dislike it much, until we got to a part about a young girl who tried to commit suicide by drowning herself in a river. She was subsequently saved and then scolded for trying to do so. That part didn't affect me that much; I decided that I could handle it. But in class the next day, our teacher told us about how suicide was a major theme in the book. Of course, the class then discussed suicide and their opinions on it, while I tried to keep a poker face. I was just sitting there picturing my dad hanging in the closet but I tried so hard to keep it together. Then, my teacher told us how she thought suicide was the stupidest thing anyone could do. She also explained to us that the rest of the book dealt with suicide a lot and we should be prepared to read tons more about it. As everyone kept talking about it I felt myself getting really hot, but I didn't crack. After class, I went to my teacher and told her about my dad. She felt awful, gave me a big hug, and told me I didn't have to read the parts about suicide in the book. It was really nice of her and I appreciated it a lot, but I'm also frustrated that I had to tell her. I wanted this year to be a fresh start, a year where I wasn't just "the student whose dad committed suicide." I wanted to know that my teachers wouldn't be biased. I wanted to just be a normal kid this year. But now I'm not, and I don't really know if it's for the better.

Saturday, October 9

It's Columbus Day Weekend and my mom and I are at our summer house with Kayla's family. Last year, this was the last trip my dad ever took with our family. He was feeling so much better, and everyone was happy, even him. He hiked a mountain with us, which we never thought he'd be able to do again. Everything seemed to be looking up. Boy, were we wrong.

I dreamed that at my summer house hundreds of people came and started trashing everything and burning fires around our house and throwing things at me and I was so scared and I was screaming for them to stop but no one was listening to me and then I saw my dad sitting in an office so I ran to him and begged him to make it stop and yelled and yelled but he just looked at me calmly, a smug look on his face that said 'I know you need me, but I'm not going to help you' and I kept pleading and he just kept looking at me with that face, and then I woke up.

I thought I was done dreaming about my dad. I thought I was at least beyond that. I feel so much better in public now but my subconscious still roams free, and I have no control over it. I try to accept that as a fact of life, and I tell myself that's okay, as long as I can control everything else then my thoughts don't matter, but I know it's all a lie, that everything's a lie, that I'm lying to myself. I don't want to lie to myself but I just want to be better. Why can't I be better?

Saturday, October 16

It's 11 months after my dad's death. It used to feel like so much longer, but now the short days make it seem like it's been much less time than that. The wounds are starting to reopen, the ones I thought I sewed up so carefully, so meticulously, and it feels like all my efforts are going to waste.

My sister is home for the weekend, and we talked about my dad. We talked about how she didn't find out about his death until the morning after it happened, and she didn't find out how it happened until the night after. I can't decide which is worse: being at college instead of there when it happened and finding out later, or being right there in the moment. I'd be so upset to know that everyone was going through this for more than 12 hours without me, while I was enjoying a carefree night with my friends. It would make me feel guilty. But she's strong, and she pulled through. She knew how to handle everything and was able to get on that plane and get herself home.

If I were in that situation, would I have been able to pull myself together like she did? How did she manage to keep herself from breaking down in front of a mass of strangers? I just don't think I have that kind of self-control like she does. But I do think that over time I will be able to regain that control. Maybe my wounds are opening a bit, but not all the way. I am still strong, and I'm not giving up. I have so much to live for, so much to prove, and nothing is going to get in my way of doing that.

What do you think?

Every situation has ups and downs, but we can always manage to pull ourselves through. For me, my wonderful friends and family helped me get through my dad's death. Think of a difficult situation you've experienced and write about what helped pull you through it.

Thursday, October 28

My dad always said he'd take me to Paris for my birthday, Bastille Day. We'd go to the celebrations and he'd tell me all about what actually happened on Bastille Day, not just common misconceptions, and we'd walk and talk and laugh and smile and it would be sunny and bright and we wouldn't worry about a thing. Because there'd be nothing to worry about, there'd just be us in our glowing utopia. We looked forward to that trip like it was something from heaven, something bigger than life that we actually thought would happen to us. That one idea represented so much more than a trip to us; it represented everything we'd ever wanted in our lives, in our thoughts, in each other, just waiting there for us to experience it. Maybe deep down we knew it would never happen, maybe that's why we could keep it so perfect and pure in our minds, because it was maybe just a little too perfect. It couldn't actually happen because it was too good to be true. That ideal vision, that ideal life that we had so carefully planned out in our brains wasn't real, it was only our imagination, our far-fetched wishes that could never come true. We knew that. We knew that we weren't the people we wanted each other to be and we knew that no fantasy could change that. We just couldn't think that, we worked our way around that so as to avoid the obvious, the elephant in the room. If we didn't actually think it then maybe, just maybe, it wasn't true, and things would work themselves out in the end.

Avoiding the truth is not the way to live. Seeing only what you want to see, pretending everything is okay when it's really, really not. You know when it's not. You can tell that something's not right. Whether you choose to listen to yourself is up to you, but you can't avoid it forever. You know yourself and your mind all too well, and you can never fully bury what you know to be true. Sooner or later, it's going to come out. And it did. My dream was shattered like a china plate falling ten stories down.

What do you think?

What's your truth? Do you find that sometimes it may be hard to accept it or believe in it?

Monday, November 1

It's November. Again. This could be the beginning of the bad feelings, the sadness, the anger, and mostly the darkness. The yelling and the pain, the fear and the despair. But not this time. This time around I'm going to fight against all of that. I'm going to build a new November, one that's so far away from my dad and my old emotions that I won't even recognize it. I won't even recognize myself because I'll move away from it all, just push it aside and proudly walk forward with my chin up and head held high, awaiting all the good things I know are going to happen to me.

I don't know how I'm going to feel in two weeks. I don't even know how I'm going to feel in two hours. That's the only thing holding me back from enjoying my new November to the fullest. I can plan out everything exactly how I want it to happen, every little detail I want, but I can't always fulfill those desires. Something can stop me. Maybe not as easily as before, though. I can deal with most of the little things that used to stop me. That's why I know deep down that I'm going to be okay no matter what, I'm going to keep fighting, and nothing and no one will hold me back.

Sometimes I go back to where I was a year ago, the dark little coiled up ball of emotion inside of me, gasping for air and trying to be heard. I feel so compressed and heavy and I just can't seem to put my finger on it, on what I'm thinking or feeling or why. Why for everything, why for every single thing, is there even a why? Maybe there's no why, maybe that's the reason I feel so lost, because I'm trying to find something that isn't there. There is no why. There's a what. There's a who. There's a where, and a how, and a when. But there just is no why.

I'm trying to put the puzzle pieces together, and I sometimes think I've gotten it, but I don't think I have it quite yet. I think I'm still working on it. And that's okay. Because I have my mom, and my friends, and my sister to help me figure it out, no matter how long it takes.

What do you think?

Is there something you're trying to understand like putting puzzle pieces together?

Write about your experience.

Friday, November 5

I'm thinking about him more frequently now, but I'm not missing him. It's just the image of him in my head, a glum, motionless picture, nothing more. I don't hear him yelling at me or anything. When I'm alone the image seems more prominent, and as the date of the anniversary comes near I really, really don't want to be alone. I don't want to come home to an empty, dark November house, on a Monday, with all the lights off, and no one home ... .

I'm not missing him though, because I know how much worse it would be if he were here. This time last year was the worst time of my life, with constant yelling and scariness and feeling very small. Now I can just be myself with no one judging and criticizing me. It is kind of lonely with only my mom and me, but it's better than my other reality, the reality that was so bad I wanted it all just to be a bad dream.

It does sort of feel like a dream now, because I feel so detached from it all. It's like my little reverie that I can try to push aside, with all the other nightmares I've had. Now, this is my new life, this is my new chapter and I'm only moving forward.

What do you think?

Describe your new life.

Tuesday, November 16

Exactly one year ago, an event happened that changed my life completely. I was utterly shocked and it felt like my whole world was turned upside down. I didn't know how to feel, what to say, or what other people were thinking about me, and I just felt so lost and helpless. I felt like there was no way out.

Now I am a very different person. I know what I'm feeling, I know what I want to say, and I don't care what people are thinking. I know how to handle my feelings and now I know that it's okay to feel them, even if I think it's not. No one's judging me, anyway. I can see things from a clearer, broader perspective. I know that it takes time to heal. You can't just expect to get over something like that in a month. It's really a process. And it continues to be a process every single day. But now all of those feelings aren't as prominent for me, and everything else in my life is much more important. I'm able to remember my dad without dwelling on him, and I can live in the present. I have amazing friends, I have an amazing mom, and I finally have myself. I've finally made peace with my emotions and I can accept them.

My life will never be the same. Nothing will ever be able to fill the void left by my dad's suicide. But I don't necessarily need it filled. I can live without him and embrace what is happening right now, in the present, and forever.

About two weeks before my dad died, he said to me, "No matter what happens, remember that I'll always love you."

I love you too, Dad.

If your heart is in Social-Emotional
Learning, visit us online.

Come see us at
www.InnerchoicePublishing.com

Our web site gives you a look at all our other Social-Emotional
Learning-based books, free activities, articles, research, and
learning and teaching strategies. Every week you'll get a new
Sharing Circle topic and lesson.

INNERCHOICE Publishing
15079 Oak Chase Court
Wellington, FL 33414

Made in the USA
Lexington, KY
30 April 2013